How to be the Parent-in-Law your kids will love

Gwynedd & Jill Harding-Jones

Acknowledgments

Many thanks to all the couples who have shared their in-law experiences with us. This book would not be what it is without you.

Copyright © 2015 by Gwynedd Harding Jones & Jill Harding-Jones

First Edition 2015

Revised 2022

Streetlamp Publishers

streetlamppublishers@gmail.com

ISBN: 978 0 9934165 0 7

Dedicated To Our

Children And Their Spouses.

Contents

Introduction

If you are a parent-in-law looking for help on how to strengthen your relationship with your child and their spouse, then this book will help you. Your relationship may have grown cold and has become strained, so you're looking for a resource that can help you start to turn things around. Or it may be you are just starting out on your journey as a parent-in-law, and are eager to make sure you make the best possible start. On the other hand, you may already be enjoying a good relationship with your in-law children and are simply looking at ways you can strengthen the relationship even further. Whatever your reason for wanting to be a better parent-in-law, this book will help you.

The first step to becoming an excellent parent-in-law is to first of all understand the *principles involved* in the in-law relationship. The second step is to then know *how to apply* those principles so that everybody in the relationship is given the best possible opportunity to flourish together. This book balances both of those two essential elements - it explains the important dynamics that need to be considered in the relationship; as well as offering practical advice and tips as to how those principles can be worked out in practice.

1

Included throughout the book are some true 'life stories' - both positive and negative. They are drawn from our own experiences, as well as the experiences of others as we've discussed the issue of parents-in-law with them over the years. Some of these stories are sad, and some are funny. They're included to help illustrate some of the problems that can arise, as well as the sorts of things to avoid in the parent-in-law relationship. Hearing the accounts of other people's experiences helps us to grow in the relationship we have with our own in-law children.

The parent-in-law relationship is unique, and is *unlike any other human relationship*. It brings its own set of distinct challenges on the one hand, while all the time offering its own set of rich rewards on the other. If we don't know how to get through the challenges, then we won't experience the rewards this relationship can bring. As we come to understand what the challenges are, and then learn how to navigate them in the best possible way, we can become parents-in-law who are loved by their in-law children, and are encouraged to be a meaningful part of their lives. We appreciate your 'in-law relationship' is unique to you and to you alone, but as you continue to read this book we believe you will glean valuable insight into what makes a good parent-in-law, so that you too will become the parent-in-law your kids will love!

Chapter 1

The Journey Begins

Over the years, we've needed to put effort into the relationships we have with our two children and their spouses. The positive relationships we now enjoy haven't just 'happened' - we've had to navigate times when there has been sharp disagreement, times when tears were shed because of words spoken, as well as times of real frustration. By learning how to navigate these difficult times successfully, we've managed to come through to the place where the relationship is stronger than it was before the challenge presented itself. This is the hope we want to pass on to those who are reading this book.

Working to overcome the obstacles the in-law relationship brings is worth the effort, because there is a joy and a reward the other side of the challenge. If we know what to do when a relationship is tested, and then apply what we know in a consistent way and to the best of our ability, we will be doing our part in building a strong in-law relationship. *Every* in-law relationship faces difficulties, because there is no perfect parent-in-law, nor are there any perfect children-in-law. Challenges are therefore bound to come no matter how good the relationship appears to be on the surface. What this book aims to do is not only help parents-in-law navigate these difficult times, but also to help bring an understanding of the dynamics of the relationship so that some of the problems which may arise can be avoided in the first instance!

Experience is a Great Teacher

The things we've learned over the years regarding what makes a good parent-in-law have come to us from two different directions. Firstly, from what we ourselves experienced with our own parents, because both sets of parents-in-law related to us in very different ways. One set of parents were generous and supportive; the other (the mother-in-law) was interfering and controlling. Though negative and extremely difficult to manage at the time, we learned first-hand some valuable lessons regarding how a parent-in-law can make life difficult for a young married couple. The painful negative experiences have been as valuable to us as the positive ones were, because they've equipped us to avoid repeating the same mistakes with our own married children and spouses.

The other direction we've learned from, and continue to learn, is in our relationships with our own children and their spouses. Though we were equipped to some degree by the experience with our own parents-in-law, we've still needed to learn from the challenges that have come up with our own children and their spouses. Our primary goal as parents-in-law is always to give our children and their spouses the freedom they need to grow in their own relationship. We're constantly learning how to play a supportive role in their lives so they can flourish to become their best. As we've given them freedom and support, we've noticed how they invite us to be part of their lives, because they value what we can bring into the relationship we have with them.

You are reading this book because you too want to be a relevant and valued part of the life of your child and spouse. You have the potential within you to become the best parent-in-law you can be, and this book will help you take steps that will bring you closer to your goal. This book helps parents-in-law understand the role they have; the responsibility they carry within the relationship; as well as equipping them to grow stronger relationships with their children and spouses.

Shared Responsibilities

Without key things in place, in-law relationships can be problematic from the outset. This book highlights some of the basic values that will help the in-law relationship be loving, enjoyable and strong right from the start. Having said that, it is important to also acknowledge not all of the responsibility for a good 'in-law' relationship lies with the parents.

Because the parent/s-in-law are the older and (hopefully) more mature side of the relationship, the responsibility *to take the lead* in building a healthy relationship rests primarily on their shoulders. But the son or daughter-in-law also have a responsibility because they too need to be prepared to play their part in developing a strong relationship. This can sometimes be difficult especially if they are immature, or have come into the family carrying their own hurts or insecurities. We need to be aware of this 'dual responsibility' so that we're not hard on ourselves (or them) when things are challenging.

New People Bring New Challenges

When someone new joins the family it becomes a totally new experience for everybody. Adding someone with different ideas, different values, and often from a different background into a family has the potential to stir things up a bit. If however we're equipped and know what the important principles are regarding welcoming someone new into the heart of the family, then we have the best possible chance of seeing a smooth transition so that the whole family can grow together - albeit in a different way to how things were previously.

If you are on the verge of welcoming a new member into your family in the form of a son or daughter in-law, then this book will help you get off to a great start. In the same way the real journey to becoming a good parent can only begin once a child is born, the journey to becoming a good parent-in-law can only really begin when a son or daughter-in-law is introduced into the family. It's important to do some groundwork, but we can't *fully* prepare ourselves until it actually happens. Making sure we start in the best possible way will give this new relationship every opportunity to grow and to flourish right from the beginning, so that everybody benefits.

You may however be further down the road as far as your relationship with your child and their spouse is concerned, and don't have the luxury of knowing what you should have done at the start of the journey. Don't worry, because even if your relationship with your child and spouse has become strained and difficult, this book will help you identify areas where things may have gone wrong, which in turn will help you take steps to remedy and repair the relationship.

Hiding is Sometimes the Easiest Option

We'll bring this chapter to a close with the true story of a young mum who struggled with her mother-in-law:

7

The mother had never accepted her son's choice regarding the woman he had married - partly because there were cultural and language differences, but also because the daughter-in-law had 'dared' to stand up to the mother-in-law early on in her marriage. Over the years the relationship between the young married couple and his mother became strained. Visiting his parents became an increasingly difficult experience because they never knew what negative comment or remark would come their way. There is a particular incident (which happened on a number of occasions) that makes this young couple laugh when they recall it, which is when the mother-in-law would turn up for an 'unannounced' visit at the young couple's house.

The mother-in-law would turn up at a time when she knew the husband (i.e. her son) was out at work. Luckily for the daughter-in-law, she had a clear view of the street in front of their house so whenever she saw his mother approaching from round the corner, she would quickly get the two young children excited at the prospect of playing a game with a ball - but in a room at the back of the house. She also took the dog with them to give the impression there was nobody at home. Once they had removed themselves as far away from the front door as they could, she would tell the children the game needed to be a 'quiet game'. They didn't realize it was so that their grandmother would think there was no one in. The mother-in-law would come to the door; she would knock, and then go on her way when there was no reply.

In one way this is a funny story, but in another, it is extremely sad. What leads a young wife with two small children to hide from her mother-in-law? The answer is very simple - there was no relationship between them. The young mum had tried to work on the relationship over the years out of respect for her husband, but sadly little changed. Everybody lost out in this relationship - the young mum; her husband because he was constantly trying to balance things; the children; as well as the mother-in-law.

Things had happened leading up to this breakdown in relationship - boundaries had not been set; issues had not been dealt with; tensions remained unresolved. Both sides had made mistakes. Because nobody within the relationship understood any of the principles that are involved in building a strong and loving in-law relationship, nothing ever changed. We are convinced however that if this mother-in-law had known what we are about to share in this book, things would have turned out a whole load better for everybody.

(At the end of each Chapter are some 'Questions to Consider'. These are optional, but in order to make full use of the book, we would suggest you find somewhere quiet where you will not be disturbed, and then take time to think about, and then answer the questions as honestly and truthfully as you can).

Questions to Consider

1. Make a list below of five words that best describe your relationship with your 'in-law children' (your child and their spouse). E.g. cold / close / struggling / growing etc.

1.

2.

3.

4.

5.

2. If you are not already enjoying it, write a sentence that describes the type of relationship *you would like to have* in the future with your in-law children.

3. What is the one positive thing you can do at this stage to take you closer towards the relationship you desire to have with your child and spouse? Make a note of it below and act on it as soon as you can.

Chapter 2

Acceptance

One of the subjects that consistently comes up when we speak to young couples about their in-laws is their desire to be accepted by their new parents-in-law. They want to be accepted for who they are, not for who the parents-in-law want them to be. It's so prominent in the discussions, that we believe acceptance needs to be high on the list of priorities that parents-in-law need to get right.

Accepting our son or daughter's choice of spouse or partner at the earliest possible stage, lays a foundation for an in-law relationship that has the potential to grow and develop into a strong and loving relationship. A lack of acceptance on the other hand, where the parents convey the sense that the spouse or partner is not good enough for their child, is potentially a *relationship killer*. At best it will stop the relationship from developing past the place of cordiality, and at worse, it can destroy the in-law relationship before it even starts.

Looking Inward

The sooner we recognize the importance of accepting our child's choice of spouse or partner, and then act on it, the better. Obviously, there are situations where it is unreasonable and even impossible to accept our child's choice, so we'll touch on that a little later in the chapter.

Ideally, accepting who our child chooses needs to start even before there is any suggestion the relationship may develop into something longer-term. As parents, it's important to identify any potential barriers that exist *within us* that can prevent us from being accepting. These may include personal prejudices relating to the race, background, personality, or appearance of the individual. It may be that we're carrying a sense of disappointment because our child's choice of spouse may not have been what we'd hoped for. If we've had expectations regarding what *we* would have liked to see in a prospective son or daughter-in-law, and they're not met in the person our child chooses, a negative and unwelcoming attitude can spill over into how we relate to them, which is extremely damaging. This is what happened to our friend who shares his story a little later on in this chapter.

If we recognize we're carrying any of these wrong attitudes, then we <u>have to lay them aside</u> for our own good, *as well as for the good of the relationship.* If we're prepared to put effort into getting to know our prospective son or daughter-in-law, even if we have some reservations, there's a strong possibility we'll be pleasantly surprised to see the *qualities* they have far outweigh the unrealistic expectations we may have put on them in the first instance. We therefore need to make sure we demonstrate our acceptance as early on in the relationship as possible, because a lack of acceptance at the beginning is lost ground that proves difficult to reclaim in later years.

Acceptance is…..

So what is acceptance and how does it work out in practice for the parent-in-law? One of the dictionary definitions of acceptance is *'the action of consenting to receive or undertake something offered'[1].* That definition puts a responsibility on the parents to either *receive* what's being offered (our child's choice of spouse / partner), or to *reject* it. There is no middle ground when it comes to acceptance. If we choose not to accept something, by default we are rejecting it. If a parent gives the impression they do not accept their child's choice of spouse, they are rejecting the very person their child loves and wants to spend their life with. We shouldn't be surprised therefore if our relationship with the young couple does not develop into something meaningful.

Count The Cost

A lack of acceptance can lead to some serious consequences. Whether they are aware of it or not, at some stage the son or daughter will be forced into a position of having to choose where their loyalty lies - is it with their parent/s, or is it with the one they love and have chosen as a life-long companion? Without a doubt, the biggest potential losers in situations like this are the parents-in-law themselves!

The cost of not accepting their child's choice goes beyond missing the opportunity to build a meaningful relationship with a new son or daughter-in-law. It also includes missing out on *everything* that comes with that relationship, e.g. grandchildren. In addition, the relationship with their own child will also suffer. All these damaging outcomes come as a result of a lack of acceptance on the part of the parent-in-law.

The other dictionary definition of acceptance is *'the process or fact of being received as adequate, valid, or suitable'*[1.]. If we look at it from the perspective of the new son or daughter-in-law, a lack of acceptance means they will see themselves as *inadequate* and *unsuitable*. What hope is there of building a relationship that is meaningful under those circumstances? Not much!

14

Give Them a Freedom to Choose

Acceptance of the person our child has chosen is important because that person is *their* choice. We may have reservations regarding their choice, but if we want to maintain the relationship we have with our child, and then go on to build a relationship with the person they have chosen, it is important to be accepting as early as possible. Though it can often be challenging, we have to respect the right of our children as individuals to make their own life choices once they become adults.

Hopefully the wisdom to make good choices and decisions will have been taught from an early age. This will help them as they step out to make big decisions, including who they want to be in relationship with on a long-term, lifetime basis. As parents we have to 'let go' and learn to take a step back as our children make their own choices. Balancing this with letting our children know we are there for them, even when we disagree with some of the choices they make, is also important. A number of in-law relationships fall at this first hurdle of acceptance, with the result that the relationship loses the potential to grow any further. It reaches an impasse where it cannot grow beyond cordial respect. Things could be so different however, simply by the parents first of all understanding the importance of acceptance, and then making every effort to exercise it to the best of their ability.

A Personal Failure

This is an area I (Jill) failed in when our daughter first started dating her (now) husband. When the relationship was in its infancy our daughter remembers specifically the advice I gave her - *'don't get romantically involved with him'!* My only defense is that I didn't understand then what I understand now regarding the importance of acceptance. The reservations I had at the time that prompted me to vocalize my concerns have since disappeared, because he has grown to be an excellent choice of husband for our daughter because he clearly loves her. I'm glad she didn't take my advice, and rather than it being a contentious issue, thankfully all of us can now see the funny side of what I said. Both of us have grown to love our son-in-law because of the genuine love and kindness he demonstrates towards our daughter, as well as towards us.

Disapproval Can Kill In-Law Relationships

Because of the bond between parents and their children, a child is acutely aware of what their parents are thinking if they make wrong choices. Children often want to please their parents, and so they can start feeling guilty if they make choices they know their parents disapprove of. If the child is weak and lacks confidence in making decisions, they may even make wrong choices in order to appease their parent's disapproval - which can have disastrous consequences.

The following is a true story that affirms the destructive effect a lack of acceptance can bring, both on the in-law relationship itself, but also for the young couple caught in the middle. By sharing this experience, we hope it will send a clear warning to all parents-in-law regarding how important it is to be accepting of their child's chosen spouse or partner.

"Even though I have been married for over 30 years, I have never felt accepted by my wife's parents. They were never particularly supportive of our marriage, and a number of incidents left me feeling they didn't believe I was worthy of marrying their daughter. I had, in a somewhat old-fashioned manner asked my future father-in-law's permission to marry his daughter and was surprised when he said "no". After some persuasion from his daughter, as well as making it clear to him that we would marry with or without his permission, he eventually relented but was never enthusiastic about the prospect of having me as a son-in-law. We moved on from that incident and continued to make plans for a church wedding in (my then) girlfriend's home village, followed by a reception in her parents' garden. The damage had already been done however, and it has been difficult for me to shake off the feeling that resulted from this initial rebuff, which was that I was never good enough to marry their daughter.

Shortly before the wedding I received a phone call from my future mother-in-law. She was emotional but to the point: "You have no right to come between a loving mother and daughter" she said. I don't recall the rest of the conversation, but that phrase has stayed with me for over 30 years. There is no 'good' time to get a phone call like that from a future parent-in-law, but what made this one even more difficult was the personal turmoil I was experiencing in my life at the time. I had finished university the previous year and was spending time with my mother and young sister following my father's death only a couple of months earlier. It was a particularly traumatic time for us all - he was still a young man (late 40's) when he died, so a phone call like that was particularly difficult for me to handle. I spoke to my girlfriend about what her mother had said. She was dismissive regarding the incident and said that the arrangements had been made and everything would go ahead as planned. She didn't take it too seriously.

After the wedding ceremony, a reception was held in my parents-in-law's garden. When it came to the time for the father of the bride to give his speech, he was unable to deliver his words because he was drunk. The speech was incoherent, and although there was some amusement from our families there was a sense of disappointment and embarrassment. He didn't have a drink problem and I've never seen him in such a state since. It was put down to nerves, but I felt his actions had devalued the occasion.

Our early-married life was characterized by frequent emotional phone calls to my wife from her mother. She (my wife) was often upset when I returned home from work because her mother had been unpleasant to her, demanding she return home (her parents lived about 250 miles away). Her father and brother would sometimes also phone in support of her mother. We both felt that her mother (who manipulated people with her charm) was behind these "urging" conversations.

The situation did start to improve after our first child was born in the mid 1980's. My parents-in-law moved closer to us so they could be closer to the grandchildren. Whether this was the real reason for their move I will never know, but I was pleased that affairs had become easier and was relieved that a major source of anxiety for my wife had now been alleviated. My subsequent relationship with her parents was civil, but never close. I always felt that I had failed to make the grade as far as they were concerned, but never quite knew why. I even felt at times they disliked me. One of the knock-on effects this had on me was that I was determined to prove myself to them, to try to make myself worthy. That was good in some ways, bad in others. I did some stupid things just to try to impress them but never succeeded.

It was impossible to discuss the situation with my wife because her relationship with her parents was improving, so she really just wanted to let sleeping dogs lie. I wasn't inclined to push it too far with her either, because I wanted to avoid upsetting her so the whole situation was an unhealthy one. This meant we never really discussed what went wrong in our relationship with her parents, which in turn meant that I have lived with a certain feeling of inadequacy throughout our married life.

My experience with my parents-in-law has made me aware of a level of selfishness that I'd never previously experienced. This was highlighted even more by the fact that my own family just weren't like that. Because I lost my father at an early age it would have been a tremendous help to me to have had a trusted older man to talk to and to bounce ideas off. Unfortunately, my father-in-law simply wasn't interested or able to be that person, in fact he was the very opposite. He responded to my vulnerability by point-scoring and fueling his fragile ego with snide remarks and little put-downs. Any ideas I came up with were quickly disregarded as insignificant and so I gave up trying in the end and built my life around others who I could trust. I came to the place where I felt my parents-in-law couldn't be trusted, which meant I was forever on my guard in my dealings with them as I had lost all respect for both of them."

How sad that a man in his fifties has been influenced by his parents-in-law to the extent that he's carried a dark cloud over himself, as well as his marriage for over thirty years. This testimony is a sobering reminder of the influence and power parents-in-law have on their in-law children.

Acceptance Is Not a Feeling - It's a Choice

Acceptance does not mean we have to agree with everything the person stands for, because that would be unreasonable. Acceptance *does* mean however that despite our differences and reservations, we make a deliberate choice to embrace *the individual* for the sake of the relationship.

I am the eldest of four children and my mum has often said she loves her in-law children very much, but could not live with any of them. She's able to say that because she has understood the choice of partner is ultimately the child's, and needs to be respected as such. They are the one who has to live with their choice, and 'do life' with them on a day-to-day basis.

The Challenging Situations

What about the situations where it is extremely difficult, unreasonable, or even impossible to accept our child's choice of spouse - what then? What if our child has clearly made a wrong choice with regard to who they are forming a relationship with - are we still expected to be accepting?

The first thing we should do is check our motivation - because the reasons for not being willing to accept our child's choice of a partner / spouse need to be *valid reasons*. We need to make sure we're not using

21

personal preferences, opinions, prejudices, or failed expectations as an excuse for not being accepting.

As parents, our natural instinct is to protect our children from harm. If it becomes clear our child's choice of partner risks damaging them, then we need to make sure we are positioning ourselves in a place of being available when they need our help. This is why it is essential to keep lines of communication open at all times, so that we can remain in a position to support, as well as able to influence the situation towards good. Once we choose to remove ourselves from the relationship (for whatever reason), we effectively lose our opportunity to be a positive influence in that particular situation.

A Mother-in-Law's Testimony

We'll share with you a very personal and honest account of an experience that has been shared with us relating to the issue of acceptance. This lady struggled with the choice her son had made, but we will let her tell her own story:

"I have three children - a son who is the eldest, as well as two daughters. With regard to my son, I would describe him as a steady, reliable, and loyal sort of boy. He has always been the serious type, so I've always thought he could do with someone who would lighten him up a bit, preferably someone who didn't have any problems of their

own! The girl he chose (though I suspected she chose him) was not that ideal person I had hoped for. I already knew her quite well and so already had my reservations about her. She had a difficult temperament. Without realizing it, I began to set myself against her, and I went as far as telling my son I did not think she was right for him. I strongly felt she would be better off in a different family than ours - a family who would like her! All of this time my son kept silent and didn't share with me what was going on in his mind.

Then a close friend invited me round to her house and told me straight that I had better come to terms with the relationship because how I felt about it wasn't going to change anything. She told me the relationship was going to happen irrespective of how I felt. Because she knew me so well she had picked up on the negative attitude I had towards my son's girlfriend and so told me that if I didn't accept the situation, I would lose the relationship I had with my son. I knew she was right, and I began to realize I had already overstepped the mark even though the relationship was in its early days. She (my son's girlfriend) had also by now realized I didn't like her. It was when my friend shared with me what she could see, that I started to back off, as well as begin to make a deliberate effort to build a relationship with my son's girlfriend.

They have now been married for a number of years and I have learned to accept my son's choice as to the girl he wanted to 'do life' with. That acceptance on my part has helped make the relationship I have with her much easier. Over the last 20 years or so I have had to work hard at building the relationship and have tried my best to repair the damage I had done at that early stage.

Even though she can be irritating at times, I have realized that I need to continue to do my best to build the relationship. I have definitely seen positive changes in her as she has matured over the years. She has grown to be a good wife to my son, as well as an excellent mother to my grandchildren. Over time, both of us have learned to respect each other, and we can now relax and have a joke in each other's company. It has taken time & effort, but it has been worth it. If I had not made the (difficult) decision to accept her as my son's choice, I would probably not have a relationship with her at all now, which in turn would have affected the relationship I have with my son, as well as with my lovely grandchildren. I will be forever grateful to my true friend who made me examine myself and helped me turn things around before it was too late."

Everybody Is Different!

Differences will always come - they may be cultural, they may be based on faith, background, language etc. If we want to be a good parent-in-law, then we have to make a deliberate choice to be accepting for the sake of the relationship. Understanding we have a freedom to embrace *the person*, without necessarily having to embrace what they believe and how they think, makes accepting our child's choice much easier. If we can embrace _the person_ our son or daughter has chosen, and then start to build a meaningful relationship with them, out of that relationship will come opportunities to talk about the differences in beliefs and views we may have!

[1.] www.oxforddictionaries.com

Questions to Consider

1. Be honest with yourself - have you truly accepted the choice your child has made regarding their spouse?

2. If not, is there a danger you are communicating this to both of them without realizing it?

3. What can you do to recover the situation so that the relationship can be restored? Do you need to consider apologizing? Saying sorry will take courage on your part, but the respect gained will last a lifetime, and will be the starting point to healing the relationship.

Chapter 3

Letting Go

Alongside the need to accept our child's choice of spouse or partner, is the need to *'let go'*. In building a strong and meaningful in-law relationship with our children and their spouses, we need to be willing to *let go* of our child (whether son or daughter) into the arms of the person they have chosen.

We know of a young couple, early on in their relationship, who were out for a celebratory meal with the young man's parents. The evening started well but when the food arrived it became obvious there was a problem with the meal that the mother had been served. She started making quite a fuss, so in an attempt to remedy the situation her son tried to sort the problem out. His girlfriend, slightly perturbed there was so much fuss over such a small issue suggested that perhaps he was making too big a deal of things. When the mother heard this, she looked at the girlfriend and said *"my dear, he will still be fussing over me long after you are gone"*. Not a good start by the mother-in-law! Not surprisingly, the evening took a slightly different direction after that and unfortunately is still remembered as one that was awkward, rather than celebratory.

The young couple went on to get married and are still married nearly 40 years later, but not surprisingly the incident clouded the in-law relationship from that time onwards. The problem was that the young man's mother had not reached the place where she realized she needed to let go of her son. That in turn shaped how she saw his new girlfriend (who later became his wife). Rather than see her qualities, she saw her as someone who would take her son away from her. Without realizing it, the girlfriend had become a source of resentment for her, which carried on into their married life.

Parents _have_ to make adjustments in their relationship with their child once their child gets married. If parents don't make the adjustments that are needed, it will lead to problems in the in-law relationship from an early stage. We'll touch on some of these problems in a moment.

A New Identity

One of the most important things for a parent to understand when their child gets married is how the *primary identity* of their child changes. Because of the new person in their lives, the title 'daughter' or 'son' is no longer the *primary* identity of the child - their

28

primary identity becomes 'husband' or 'wife', and they need to be respected as such. Once a parent understands this truth, and then accepts it as a something which inevitably happens when a child gets married, it becomes easier for them to accept the situation. Efforts can then be directed towards edifying their child's new identity, rather than trying to hold on to the old.

It is extremely sad when parents try to hold on to the only identity they have known for their child - a son or a daughter, and fail to release their child into their new identity as a 'husband' or 'wife'. When this happens, the now married child becomes trapped because they are being pulled in two directions by trying to be faithful to both parties (husband on one side, parents on the other). This then has a knock-on effect on their spouse, because they become increasingly frustrated at the lack of freedom the parents-in-law are giving them.

An underlying tension begins to build up for the young couple as a result of the parents-in-law exerting pressure, with the result they may start arguing about the expectations the parents-in-law are putting on them. Not letting go of their child is often a reason parents-in-law are such a contentious issue for young married couples. Things could be so different if only the parent-in-law simply recognized the need to 'let go' of their child, and then work at supporting the young couple, rather than giving them reasons to experience divisions by arguing.

It is difficult for some parents, especially those who have an insecure and controlling personality, to accept that their child has someone more important in their lives than them. This is a common reason why relationships between parents and their in-law kids do not grow into something meaningful. This is what happened to the friend who shared his experience in the previous chapter. The emotional phone call from his future mother-in-law saying he had *"no right to come between a loving mother and daughter"* shows the tragic consequences of what can happen when a parent is not willing to let go of their child.

Just to reassure any parent who may be anxious about the thought of *'letting go'* of their child - the child *still remains* a son or daughter once they are married, it is just that this is no longer their *primary* identity. First and foremost they are now a husband or a wife because of their choice to make someone else the most important person in their lives. Our personal experience has been that by letting go, we have received far more back from our in-law children than we could ever have hoped for - but we wouldn't have experienced it if we weren't prepared to let go in the first instance!

'Who Gives this Woman to be Married to this Man?'

Most of us are familiar with the vicar or pastor asking the question *'who gives this woman to be married to this man?'* as they're officiating the wedding ceremony. The father of the bride usually responds on behalf of both parents and then places the hand of his daughter into the hand of the groom. This is a highly symbolic moment, because it signifies the parent/s *'giving away'* their daughter in marriage to their chosen partner. Seeing it only as a tradition devalues the powerful statement this act is designed to bring - it is meant to be the statement of how the parents are agreeing to let go, and 'hand over' their child to someone else. Traditionally this only happens with the bride, but we believe it is equally important for the groom also to be 'handed over'. One way is to simply include a simple declaration by the groom's parents within the ceremony, saying they are freely releasing their son to his new bride.

The 'giving away' of our child is not easy because we are giving away someone who is very precious to us. If this simply remains as part of a marriage ceremony without a conscious and heart-felt decision on the part of the parents, then there's a possibility the in-law relationship will struggle for many years to come. Once the decision to willingly give our child to someone whom they love has been made however, *it's important to remember they don't stop being our son*

31

or daughter. It's just that by releasing them to their spouse, they're being given the freedom to become who they want to become in the context of the new relationship they are committed to.

Keeping Hold Is Destructive

Trying to keep hold of our adult child by not giving them a freedom to grow in their new identity as a husband or wife can have a number of serious consequences, all of which are destructive. The most obvious one is the potential for a damaging division to emerge between the couple and their parents-in-law. But there is also the possibility of a division between the young couple themselves, because of the frustration and split loyalties as mentioned earlier. This is the exact opposite of what a loving parent wants for their child, which further reinforces the need to 'let go'.

There's a danger also the son or daughter-in-law will start to become increasingly frustrated at the parents-in-law, and even begin to resent them. It's difficult for a spouse to sit on the side-line watching their wife or husband being manipulated and controlled by his or her parents without reacting in one way or another. Sooner or later there will be some sort of reaction - at best it can result in minimizing contact by withdrawing from the relationship, or at worse ending up having a full-blown confrontation.

Then we've got the parents-in-law themselves. If they're still trying to hold on to their child, a sense of disappointment will start to build within them because their child and spouse are not making the choices they want them to make. This sort of attitude is obviously unacceptable, selfish, and controlling. It is easily remedied by the parents giving their child and spouse the freedom they need to make their marriage, not their parents' wishes, the main priority of their lives.

Help Them To Be Their Best

As parents, we have a role to play in helping our children become the best they can be in their new identity as a wife, or as a husband. We should take a step back, allow them to go in the direction they feel is best for them, but making ourselves available for them when they ask for our advice or help. This is a healthy attitude to take, and helps them become the best they can be in their relationship with their new spouse. As we encourage them, it shows how we as parents understand (as well as accept) that our child's spouse is now the most important person in their life. They are the ones with whom our child will find the happiness and fulfilment they are meant to enjoy - a purpose and meaning to life that parents can never give.

Closing Remarks

Simply because the child has someone more important in their lives than their parents, does not mean they love their parents any less. It just means they are entering a new season where there is a potential for the child's love towards the parents to deepen and mature - provided the parents are willing to release their child into this new season with their blessing and encouragement. Just because the child has left the family home does not mean the parents cease to be parents. The role of parents simply *changes*, and it is the parents who fail to embrace the new season ahead of them that fail to build the relationship which needs to develop in this new season. The parents who recognize and understand the need to change however, and work at making those changes, are the ones who have every opportunity to develop a healthy, loving, and meaningful in-law relationship with their child and spouse.

Questions to Consider

1. What are some of the personal challenges you have faced as a parent in releasing your child into their new role as a husband or wife?

2. Do you feel you have overcome these challenges, or are they still lingering?

3. What can you do, in your particular situation, to help yourself fully overcome the challenges you've faced, so that you're able to fully release your child (or children) into their new season in life?

Chapter 4

Opening Medley

This chapter is one of four where we bring together a collection of subjects relating to the in-law relationship. Each topic does not warrant a chapter in itself, but is nonetheless important to consider. These are again drawn from of our own personal experiences, the experiences of our friends, as well as some young couples who have shared with us the challenges they face with their parents-in-law.

Let Them Grow Together

The journey of life a young couple embark on when they first get married is exciting. On looking back, as we started our own journey when we first got married, we didn't realize how immature we were regarding life experience, yet we thought we knew it all! We had no idea what challenges lay ahead of us nor how to deal with them. We were probably no different to any other young couple who think they have all the answers for what life will bring.

Being a parent-in-law means we have at least some degree of life experience. Over the years every one of

37

us has grown in wisdom as we've had to face the varied challenges life can bring. We also know that our in-law children are yet to learn some of the things we already know, *but we need to avoid trying to teach them how to live their life,* because they need to learn for themselves. Hard as that may sound, if we start telling them what they should and should not do, we'll be seen as interfering, even though our motivation to help may be honorable.

Knowing when and how to give advice needs a great deal of wisdom, as does knowing when *not* to give advice! Giving and receiving advice works best out of relationship, which is why as we make growing the relationship our primary aim, we will gain their trust and confidence and they will then ask for our advice if and when they need it. Giving the young couple a freedom *to grow together,* allowing them to face the challenges *together,* without us trying to always give them the answers is important, because it is *their* life-learning journey. They are the ones who need to learn the lessons of how to live life as a married couple. Obviously there are times when we do need to step in and give advice without being asked, for example if we are concerned about what will happen to them. But we're not to be too eager to give our opinion on everything - otherwise it will be seen as interfering.

We acknowledge how difficult it is for parents-in-law to get the right balance between 'sitting back' doing nothing, and being seen as interfering. A young couple shared with us how they have one set of parents-in-law who 'sit back' to the extent it comes over as if they're not interested! It would be great if there were a formula to help us get this right - how to balance being helpful yet not interfering - but unfortunately there isn't! It's something we need to be aware of, and then learn how to get it right as we 'do life' with them.

Our own journey with getting the balance right between being helpful, and being seen as interfering has sometimes been a difficult one, sometimes having to learn the hard way. One set of our in-law children sees us as interfering when we try to give advice, whereas the other set is grateful that we care! As a result we take a different approach with both, having learned to adapt along the way to their different personalities. There are no hard and fast rules - this is something we have to be aware of, and then learn on the job!

Accept There Will Be Differing Values

Families are made up of individuals, with each one having a differing viewpoint regarding certain issues. Sometimes those views can be at opposite ends of the spectrum. Though challenging, this can be used to the parents-in-law's advantage if handled correctly. It can become an opportunity for us to learn how to engage with someone who doesn't necessarily agree with us, as well as an opportunity for us to learn new things, if we're prepared to listen.

Listening to other people's views is a good thing at many different levels, even if we don't necessarily agree with them. Differing viewpoints will undoubtedly exist within the in-law relationship, so we need to be very careful that diverse opinions don't lead to division between individuals (or couples). Recognizing it as an opportunity to grow, and being open to the possibility we can learn something new (even about ourselves), is a positive thing. We also need to accept that the possibility that we're right about everything doesn't exist, and so need to respect the opinions of others, making an effort to engage in a meaningful dialogue with them which doesn't result in an argument.

We can share this difficult topic without pointing a finger at anyone because our in-law children have helped us over the years recognize certain prejudices we were carrying. Though uncomfortable to hear, it gave us the opportunity to correct the way we viewed particular issues. We've learned over the years that though it can be challenging at times, having different people with different opinions is not necessarily a negative thing - but we need to make sure we're open to listening to others rather than expect others to always listen to us. Don't forget they are adults!

Don't Place Unreasonable Expectations on Your Child and Spouse

"Are we dressing for dinner?" is a frequent question that gets asked of one young couple when they visit their in-laws. They have shared with us how there is an expectation on them to dress up for dinner, every time, even when the meal is a takeaway. The young man is expected to wear smart trousers and a shirt, whilst his wife wears a dress and high heels. This is a foreign concept to the young couple who enjoy the outdoors and are most comfortable dressing casually. They have tried making a joke of the request by saying *"Yes, we will be dressing for dinner unless you would prefer us to come without clothes!"* As a further attempt at making light of the situation they have taken it to the extreme by over-dressing in outrageous outfits - but all to no avail. The lesson here is very simple - we mustn't put our own expectations on our in-law children. Appreciate them for who they are, not who we would like them to be.

Give Space and Allow for Independence

It's natural for parents who love their children to want to spend time with them. This is just as true after they have left home and are married. We need to bear in mind however that it is also natural for the young couple to want to spend time together so they can grow in their own relationship without feeling crowded. Living in close proximity can sometimes become a problem for the in-law relationship because it makes it more tempting to 'pop' in to see them as and when the desire arises - which is not always a healthy thing. From our personal perspective we try to avoid calling unannounced, without first of all checking whether it's convenient to call or not.

Again, we need to use common sense with this, but be aware of the need to honor the young couple and their necessity to spend time together without interference from their parents-in-law. We were horrified recently to hear of a situation where the parents (in-law) had their own set of keys cut, without the permission of the young couple, so they could 'pop round' whenever they wanted! Everybody needs their own space where they can close the door behind them and relax knowing it is their private place to be themselves.

We have some friends who have got this balance just right with their daughter and son-in-law. Some years ago, their first grandchild was due and everyone was very excited. The young couple had decided that once the baby was born, the husband would take a full week off work so that the new family could have some bonding time together. Although grandma and grandpa were a little disappointed that their services would not be required for this first week, they didn't want to interfere. They wanted to give the young couple their full freedom, so they held back their disappointment and did not put any pressure on them. When their new granddaughter was born, the grandparents drove for three hours to visit, and then returned home the same day as planned.

Three days later they received a call from their daughter asking if her mum would meet them at the house once she was discharged from hospital. She checked that her son-in-law was okay with this arrangement, then packed her bags once more and made the journey south. The parents-in-law (now grandparents) had recognized the young couple would need support during these first few days with their new baby, but had not forced the issue. It was a wise choice, because forcing help on them would have labeled her as an interfering mother-in-law. Responding to the request for help however was a totally different situation, and was seen as a blessing, not an interference. Their wisdom during this time played a major part in building an excellent in-law relationship with their kids that continues to this day.

Don't Interfere

A young husband came home from work very excited at an advert he had seen for a tandem bicycle he wanted to buy. The wife was less than enthusiastic but agreed to look at it, if only to keep him happy. The wife's parents-in-law happened to be visiting at the time so her father-in-law decided he wanted to come along, while the mother-in-law looked after the two young children. They agreed beforehand that the most they would pay was $100.

When the bicycle was wheeled out for inspection it became apparent that it was not built for two people – but four! There were child seats on both the front and back as well. It was so large that the wife immediately decided she DID NOT want it! Still enthused however, the husband managed to negotiate the asking price down to $110, which was still $10 over what the couple had agreed would be their maximum budget if they were going to buy it. To the young wife's great relief the owner refused to budge any lower on the price, so her heart began to lift at the prospect of returning home without the bike. Then all of a sudden the father-in-law whipped out his wallet and handed over the additional $10! The bike was duly tied to the top of the car and went home with two very excited men and one less than excited wife. Thinking he was being helpful, what the father-in-law had actually done was come between the couple, who had already decided not to go above $100. It would have been interesting to be a fly on the wall when the young couple were left alone to discuss what had just happened!

Questions to Consider

1. Is there anything in this chapter that has resonated with you regarding how you relate to your child and spouse? If there is, make a note of it below.

2. Do you need to make any changes in how you relate to your child and their spouse in this area? What are those changes, and how can you best implement them?

Chapter 5

Clear Communication

Good communication in extremely important in every relationship. We need to be aware as parents-in-law of the variety of different ways in which families communicate (or fail to communicate in some instances). This means that when someone new is introduced into the family, they may be unfamiliar with the way their new family unit communicates (or doesn't communicate), which can lead to problems. It's important to know this so that we can avoid problems arising through misunderstanding. If misunderstanding is left unchecked, it can lead to a serious breakdown of relationship. This is why we believe communication is an important subject to touch on in this book.

Friends of ours have shared with us an experience they had when they decided to visit the wife's parents over the Christmas period. This was their first Christmas after getting married, and because they didn't have a lot of money at the time it was a real sacrifice to them. Even though her parents lived a considerable distance away they decided it was the right thing to do and so headed off. The journey was long and made especially difficult because of how busy the public transport system was at that time of year - other people were also travelling for the same reason. After an extremely tiring journey over land and sea (literally), a journey that took nearly twenty-four hours, they finally arrived, exhausted.

It wasn't long after arriving that one of the girl's parents asked the husband *"don't people normally go to their own families for Christmas?"* A simple question in itself possibly, but one that could easily have been taken to mean *'what are you doing here?'* In the context of what the young couple had sacrificed with regard to time and money in order to get there, it would have been better simply to welcome them, and then to show gratitude for the effort they had made in order to spend time together over such a special time of year.

The subject of communication in and of itself is vast, but by simply sharing what we have learned over the years we hope it will help others avoid some of the difficulties we have experienced. Hopefully it will help some to start resolving issues that have surfaced as a result of poor communication. For others, we hope it will help them to start *building* a foundation early on so that their relationship with their in-law children will grow and flourish into a strong one.

What Is Communication?

Communication simply means exchanging information. Unless we've decided to live on a desert island and withdraw from the world, communication is an integral and vital part of our everyday lives. The means by which we're able to communicate are vast, but when it comes to communicating *within a relationship*, we've whittled it down to just a few so we can focus on what we see as the most important ones.

The ways we communicate within a relationship can be by text or e-mail; we can write a hand written note, or we can send a card. Though important, these methods of communication are not what we're focusing on in this chapter. Our focus is primarily on how we communicate through the words we speak and the actions we take - which includes our 'body language'. As humans, we're not limited to words when we communicate with each other, we can communicate with our eyes, with a smile, with a gentle touch. Strong emotions such as anger and tears also communicate to the other person how we're feeling and what is going on inside of us. Even silence communicates something, which can either have a positive or negative effect depending on the facial expression that goes with it!

The way we communicate with each other will often form the basis of how the other person responds to us. If we expect someone to respond to us in a positive manner, then we need to make sure our communication towards them in the first instance is positive. In highlighting these various forms of communication (which are certainly not exhaustive), it may help us to pause for a moment and ask ourselves what are we currently communicating through our words, as well as our actions?

How Do You Communicate as a Family?

Different families communicate in different ways. Some families may be used to telling each other openly and honestly exactly how they feel about a situation without the fear of thinking they will offend each other. They are used to being able to communicate their feelings clearly with no risk of damaging the relationship. This way of communicating may come as a shock to others because as a child they may not have had a freedom to openly express their feelings without the fear of being rebuked. They will have been conditioned and taught not to share what they are thinking or how they are feeling in such an open way. We're not saying this in order to make a judgement on who is right or who is wrong. We're simply bringing it to the surface so that as parents-in-law we can at least be aware of the differences (and therefore potential difficulties) that exist in the area of how individuals communicate with each other within the family unit.

Understanding that people communicate differently will help us in our approach to how we communicate with our in-law children. In addition, acknowledging the way *we* communicate may not always be positive (i.e. acknowledging we have room to grow ourselves), will also help us as we build meaningful relationships with our in-law children.

I was brought up in a family where everyone was allowed to have an opinion and we were encouraged to share it. At times this can be helpful, but at other times I've come to recognize I need to be careful, so that I share things in a more sensitive way that cannot be misunderstood. I don't always get it right, but then again I'm still on my journey of learning!

Don't Allow Emotions To Rule

What can be really challenging for all of us is when the emotions within us are rising and we're tempted to respond out of how we feel, not what we know should be the best way to respond. We've all done it, but if we're prepared to say sorry it will be the first step to reconciling the situation. It can be difficult not to allow feelings of hurt, anger, or pride to dictate how we respond. However, if we can learn to actually listen to what is being said, and then

51

respond out of a place where the relationship is the most important thing (rather than how we feel), then it will help the relationship to grow rather than be a potential cause for division.

Communicating Through Actions

Our 'body language' is one means of communication, but so also are our *actions*. With this in mind we need to be careful that what we see as one thing, is not misinterpreted by someone else as something completely different. I'll share a recent experience as an example to illustrate what I mean.

I am by nature 'a doer' - I really enjoy doing things for others. If I see something that needs doing I'll get stuck in and do it. Even though my intentions are pure because my heart simply wants to help, it has on occasions been seen as interfering. It has also been interpreted as a judgement that the other party is not doing a good job. Until this was pointed out to me, I had absolutely no idea that my willingness to 'do' was being taken in this way. I thought everybody else saw it as I saw it, namely that I wanted to help.

Unfortunately I had failed to recognize the way that I was communicating was not correct. Even though there was the temptation to get upset or offended when it was first pointed out to me, it has actually been extremely helpful to me. I have become aware that although I have a heart to help, I still need to be careful regarding what I am communicating to the other person so that it is not being taken the wrong way. It has made me think more carefully about the way I explain why I am offering to do something, so that the other person does not feel they are being criticized or judged in any way. It has also made me realize that the things I see as important are not necessarily important to others - which is okay! We all have differing ideas and it is helpful when we can understand each other's viewpoint. This is why good communication is a foundational part of building great relationships.

Think Before You Speak

How we phrase our questions, as well as our tone is also important. For example *'would you like me to give you a hand with that?'* sounds much softer than *'this is the way you should do it'*. One is asking *'do you need help?'*; the other is saying *'I have a better way of doing it.'* One is helpful in building a relationship, the other is not. We're not advocating treading on eggshells - we're simply suggesting the need to consider how we communicate with our words.

This is especially important early on in the relationship because as the relationship grows, communication becomes easier. We get to know how the other person ticks, as well as their likes and dislikes. We become more comfortable with each other and so this makes it easier to talk about issues that may be a little more contentious, as well as being in a place where any misunderstandings can be cleared up much more easily. It ultimately means the relationship is able to go to a higher level because a connection at 'heart level' begins to develop.

'The Aunty Margaret Syndrome'

This is a term we use to describe a particular way of communicating, when a person wants to say something but is hiding behind someone else's name. They will say something like *'Aunty Margaret has noticed you haven't been to visit me for a few weeks now'* or *'Aunty Margaret was saying how her children always take her out for lunch on Sundays'*.

Whether 'Aunty Margaret' really said it or not is irrelevant, the reason for saying it is in order to communicate something they themselves are not prepared to say. They are hiding behind the cloak that someone else has said it. Our advice is never to do this because your in-law kids will soon see through it and once they have recognized what you are doing, they will begin to hear everything you say through the lens of suspicion. It doesn't work anyway because they know they are not accountable to 'Aunty Margaret'! In the end, it simply means that the issue being brought to the table will never be dealt with properly.

Encouraging Through Communication

As parents we have an important role in *supporting* our children and how we communicate this support is very important. Constant negative input and criticism will lead to a feeling of failure on the child's part which in turn will damage the relationship between us and them. Because how we communicate with others is greatly influenced by our own upbringing, in some instances we will need to look carefully, and if necessary adjust how we say things. For some of us, a gentle approach does not always come easily but it can be achieved with a little practice. The saying "it's not so much what you say but how you say it" is true, and it's not a bad thing to mention again that we can 'say' things with our body language, in addition to our words.

As a married couple, we have personally needed to regularly correct each other on this point. We both acknowledge that what the other person has said has value, but the value has been shrouded by the attitude that was used in saying it. We can easily lose the importance of what we're saying if it is said with a wrong attitude. Most mums know well enough how a look will often be enough to communicate to a child without the use of words - which is a powerful truth. If we are not careful our expressions will give away our feelings without the need for words, often without us actually realizing it. It then becomes an uphill struggle to get the person we're communicating with to actually hear the heart of what we're saying.

Clear Communication Saved The Day

We had the opportunity to practice our communication skills when we lived with our daughter and son-in-law for four months whilst we were in-between houses. We purposely sat down with both of them at the beginning of our stay and asked them to be honest and upfront with us if anything cropped up that they were unhappy about. For example, if we were doing something in a way that annoyed them such as putting things in the wrong place, or staying in the shower too long, then they were to tell us. This helped all of us to know there was a freedom to be open and completely honest with each other (them more than us because it was their house).

What this meant was that instead of having a moan in private with potential issues remaining unresolved, we were all able to address certain issues that had the potential to become annoying and cause tension. Our time living with our daughter and son-in-law over this four-month period went extremely well, and we are convinced that one of the reasons for this was because we made sure the channels of communication were open right from the start.

Questions to Consider

1. Take some time to think about the following questions:

"Do my words and actions help to build relationships, or cause division?"

"Are my words encouraging, affirming and supportive, or are they critical and judgmental?"

"Does the way I communicate show that I care and help nurture, or does it say, "my way is the only way?"

2. Even if you feel you are communicating well at the moment, is there anything you can do to further improve the way you communicate so that your child and spouse know you love them, accept them, and support them?

Chapter 6

Second Medley

Be Generous With Help And Support

Our children and their spouses will at some point need our help. It could be our time or experience in helping with things like jobs around the house or decorating. It may be they need financial help if things are a bit tight for them. In our experience it is a great blessing for *us*, as well as to *them* when we are able to help. We know many parents share this whether their child is married or not.

Not only can DIY and decorating be an immediate practical help to the young couple and save them money, it is also a great opportunity to pass on skills we have acquired. If money is short, then a gift voucher, help with rent, or even a paid trip to the supermarket can go a long way to helping the young couple, especially when they are first setting out on their journey together. We need to get the balance right however and not overwhelm them with generosity. That way they can maintain their independence, and not start to feel they are being propped up my mum and dad!

Our own parents-in-law were a tremendous help to us especially early on in our marriage. They would help by doing practical jobs, as well as giving us a freedom to use their caravan home whenever we wanted. We were able to go there at a moment's notice with our young children which made a big difference to us at the time. There is great satisfaction and joy for the parents-in-law *themselves* when they're able to help and give support, but it also speaks volumes to our in-law children regarding how much we care for them.

Hold Your Tongue!

Parents have a significant input into the lives of their children as they grow up. A time comes however when parents have to back off and allow their child to learn how to make life choices for themselves. We've already touched on how important (and often difficult) it is to get the balance right between being available to give advice and wisdom, yet not interfering. Holding our tongue is part of the learning curve that parents-in-law have to learn in this area!

Holding our tongue so as not to interfere needs more practice for some than others - we've had to learn this the hard way over the years! The earlier in the in-law relationship we recognize the importance of, and then put into practice when *not* to say something, the better. Our in-law children need to know a freedom to make decisions with their spouse or partner without interference, and even a contribution that is well meaning can sometimes come across as interfering.

A friend shared a story with us about the time she visited her parent's house without her husband. She was experiencing a lot of 'back seat driving' advice from her mother whenever they were out and about in the car. She found it quite unsettling because it undermined her confidence so she decided to discuss it with her husband when she got back home.

The next time she was due to visit, the husband made sure he went with her, because he wanted to teach his mother-in-law a lesson she would never forget. With his mother-in-law in the back seat, he took over the driving. At a side road trying to pull out onto a busy main road he spotted the tiniest of gaps, so he revved the engine up as hard as he could and dropped the clutch, then shot out onto the main road, literally with the tires screeching. They made the exit onto the main road safely, but the resulting silence from the back seat has lasted to this day. The mother-in-law has never since commented on her daughter's driving.

Try Not To React Negatively To Decisions They Make

As much as we love our children, we have found there are times when we need to hold back in sharing our true feelings especially when a decision they make has a direct effect on us personally. For example, a decision to move further away (even to another country) because of job opportunities or a fresh challenge can have a massive knock-on effect for parents-in-law, especially if there are grandchildren involved.

There is no problem with sharing how we feel because that sort of decision has the potential to affect our lives greatly, but we need to be careful not to respond from a place of selfish interest. We need to do our best to give encouragement in what is positive for them (because there will obviously be good reasons why they have taken the decision). How a situation is likely to affect us personally is usually what comes to mind for us first, but if we can learn to look at the positives for them, it will help both parties to move forward. In everything, we always need to make sure we react in a way that ensures our relationship with them will have been maintained once we're the other side of whatever the challenge is.

Respect Boundaries

We've already touched on how important it is to respect our in-law children's private space - this also includes their house. When we visit them in their home, we need to remember it is their 'patch'. They make the rules not us, and so we need to respect that. If they want to do things differently to how we do things in our own home, then that's up to them. We have to respect their choices and abide by their rules whether we agree with them or not.

A personal experience we can share where this became a particular problem for us as a young married couple was when we decided we would no longer allow anybody to smoke in our house. We made the decision when our first child was born. This was over 35 years ago when cigarette smoking was much more acceptable and not as much of an anti-social issue as it is now.

Our decision had a direct impact on our parents-in-law because both sets were smokers. They had been used to having a cigarette whenever they visited us, so this was now a new situation for them. When we explained our decision, one set of in-laws accepted it, the other didn't. Unfortunately it became a controversial issue, when really it shouldn't have been. Despite the opposition we held fast to our decision, not because we wanted to make a point, but rather because we wanted to protect the health of our child.

We did win out in the end, but there were no victors really because it affected the relationship negatively. It had become easier not to extend an invite rather than have to deal with the awkwardness and friction that seemed to arise every time there was a visit. As parents-in-law we need to respect boundaries, respect their different choices, and not expect to continue to do things our way when we're asked to do things differently.

Questions to Consider

1. You may not be able to help your child and spouse financially, nor do you have the necessary skills to help them with repair jobs around the house. But what resource or skill *do* you have that can be shared with them to help them in some way? Have a think about it, and decide how best to help them.

2. How well do you respect your in-law children's *boundaries*? Do you need to make any adjustments - if so, what are they?

Chapter 7

Loving On Purpose

Knowing we are loved is a basic human need - it is a key ingredient to being able to thrive as an individual. That's why it is so important to make sure our new son or daughter-in-law know that we love them. Love adds an ingredient into the relationship that acts as a 'fertilizer', causing the relationship to bloom.

I (Jill) was brought up in a family where we all knew beyond doubt we were loved. This gave me a very secure childhood, which then overflowed into my adult life and has helped me in lots of positive ways. Over the years I have come to understand that not all families are loving - not everyone has been as fortunate as I have been. As soon as our own children were born, we made sure they knew they were loved. We now purposefully extend this love to both our son-in-law and daughter-in-law.

Love Considers Others

I do understand however that not everybody has had the positive experience of having a loving childhood that I had. When this happens, it can become more difficult for some to give, as well as to receive love. This may not always be the case, but it's worth mentioning because if we believe our son or daughter-in-law did not have the experience of a loving family, we need to be aware of it so as not to overwhelm them when they join our family. Giving hugs and kisses is a natural expression of love and affection for some, but it can be a little daunting for others if they are not used to it.

Being loving means we are warm-hearted towards our family, patient with them, and non-judgmental. It means we are kind, we are trusting, as well as generous towards them. Even though we want to be all these things to our in-law children, there are no perfect parents-in-law that always get everything right. Despite any shortcomings we may have, if the desire of our hearts is to purposely love then we will succeed!

Love Is A *Choice*, Not Just A Feeling

Being loving is made up of many different elements, *because love is more than a feeling*. Some of the ways love works out in practice is being respectful of different opinions even when we don't agree; as well as being kind and helping others in practical ways. *Once we realize love is not limited to a feeling, it means we can still love someone even if we don't feel like it.*

An example of this would be when someone hurts us, but we make the choice not to hurt them back. Instead, we choose to be kind towards them, both with our words and our actions. Even though our feelings may be trying to take us in a different direction, choosing to express kindness rather than offence is an expression of love towards that person. *The truth that we can still love someone even when we don't feel like it is so powerful it can set us free, as well as having the potential to restore damaged relationships.* Choosing to act in love, even when we ourselves are hurting, is the medicine for releasing us from negative emotions that try to lead us on a downward spiral. This downward spiral is what eventually ends up destroying relationships.

Love that considers others ahead of ourselves will always lead us to make right choices - choices that are not emotionally driven nor dictated by what is going on around us. If we can learn to make loving choices, making a priority of putting the other person at the forefront of our thinking, it will build up the relationship rather than tear it down. There is no doubt that right, loving choices bring long-term benefits for everybody in the relationship.

Loving Through Words

Words are extremely powerful 'tools' - they can be used to edify people, or they can be used to bring a person down. Encouraging someone with our words is a simply thing to do, because it builds people up, as well as the relationship. Criticizing someone is also an easy thing to do, but it has the totally opposite effect because it will eventually destroy a relationship. The words we use are effectively a barometer of what is going on inside, so in challenging family situations we need to on the one hand have a freedom to express how we feel, but on the other use our words in a way that builds the relationship up and not cause division.

True Love Is Unconditional

Love puts the other person's needs or interests first, and does not hold onto past hurts. Love is willing to forgive *and* forget. All these things show we care about the person and that the relationship we have with them is important to us. When someone has not experienced love in their own life they will often have difficulty in receiving love because they feel they don't deserve to be loved. If this is the case in our situation, we need to continue to love because the individual *will* eventually come to see that we love and accept them for who they are, not what they do. We may not agree and be comfortable with every aspect of their character, but if we wait until they fit into our mold before we show them love, then that is not love at all. This is *conditional love;* which means we are only willing to show love and affection once they please us. Conditional love is controlling and manipulative, and is not a basis to build any loving relationship upon.

Still A Work In Progress!

All of us are a work in progress as far as being able to love our in-law children perfectly is concerned. We're all on a journey, and the likelihood is that we're probably at different stages of that journey. But if we can grasp the *principle* that love is a choice and not just a feeling, then we can at least make a start towards our goal of building a loving in-law relationship. It's not a science, there is no set formula, but hopefully the *principles* we are sharing are helping people as they navigate their own journey as parents-in-law.

Start With One Small Step

As we reflect on what it means in practice to love our in-law children, we may feel overwhelmed, seeing ourselves a long way from the benchmark. Don't be discouraged, because even when we take the *smallest* of steps towards our goal, we're closer to where we're trying to get than if we hadn't taken any steps at all. We're not to be concerned about how far away we may be from the 'gold standard'; our concern should be whether or not we have taken the first step towards purposely loving our in-law children.

Without exception, every one of us has the ability to take a step towards loving our in-law children, no matter how small that step is, if we choose to do so.

Before we move on to the next chapter its worth sharing the following testimony about a loving mother-in-law. This account clearly demonstrates how *it is* possible to be a parent-in-law your kids will love!

"My mother just loved him (the son-in-law). We always smile when we remember her. She was by our side when we needed her but maintained her independence at the same time – she balanced this brilliantly. She joined in the melee of family life and when she came on holiday with us, she didn't flinch the time we floated down the Dordogne in a rubber raft with our youngest child in a buggy, and the older children wearing armbands! Another memorable occasion we fondly recall is the time we couldn't find a hotel room when we were on holiday, again in France. We all slept in the back of our battered old car only to wake up in the morning in the middle of a French market - we had picked the main square to park up for the night! She took it all in her stride, she was just warmth and sunshine and we miss her even now."

What a wonderful legacy this lady left for her daughter and son-in-law!

1. Take some time to think about the ways you *already* demonstrate love to your child and spouse - especially with the words you speak and the things you do for them. Make a list of as many things as you can think of to encourage yourself.

2. What other things could you do that would give a clear demonstration to them that you love them?

Chapter 8

Extending Forgiveness

Forgiveness is a powerful expression of what it means to love. None of us are perfect, which means we all have the potential to get hurt as a result of things that have been said or done. When that happens within the context of a relationship, forgiveness has to be employed so that the relationship can be restored. One side of the relationship needs to *extend* forgiveness, the other needs to *receive* it.

Relationships often break down because of a *lack* of forgiveness. When things happen within relationships to cause offence, rather than reconciling the relationship through forgiveness, the division widens over time because offence is given opportunity to grow. You may find this has happened with your in-law relationship after something was said or done, even innocently. It hasn't been dealt with properly, and so has grown to cause a division. What should you do when this happens?

The starting point towards reconciliation is to understand what forgiveness is, and then to be willing to either freely *give* forgiveness, or *receive* forgiveness depending on the situation. Either way, forgiveness is an essential key to healthy relationships, which unfortunately some people are unaware of and so their relationships never get restored when someone is offended.

The Fruit of Taking Offence is Unpleasant

Taking offence at what someone says or does causes a division between the two parties. Unless that offence is dealt with through forgiveness, it will continue to grow in either one, or both parties involved. Eventually the fruit of taking offence will become visible. Bitterness, anger, and resentment regarding what was said or done will continue to brew under the surface if left unchecked. The relationship then becomes superficial, or worse still divided to the degree that eventually there is no relationship at all. Even the once-loving relationship between the child and their parents is at risk, because the child wants to remain loyal to their spouse. Everybody loses out when offence is not dealt with through forgiveness.

What Is Forgiveness?

Understanding what forgiveness actually is, is simple. It is the *practice* of forgiving someone that is the difficult part. In essence, forgiveness means *making a conscious decision to let go of the offence caused.* This is the result of recognizing the relationship with the person who has caused the offence is more important than holding on to the offence. It's also recognizing we're tired of carrying the fruit that offence brings; realizing it's doing more damage to us than the other person. Forgiving somebody does not mean denying we have been hurt; nor does it ignore the fact that an injustice has been suffered. Despite the hurt and pain we feel as a result of the offence, we're *choosing* to consciously let go of it because the relationship we want with the other person is more important to us. It's being prepared to take a step towards reconciling the relationship, at a cost to ourselves. If the relationship is important, then we will be willing to pay the price to forgive.

Feelings Try to Stop Forgiveness

Just like love in the previous chapter, forgiveness is not a feeling - it's a choice. The feelings of injustice, the feelings of anger and bitterness will try to stop us extending forgiveness. If we wait until we *feel* like forgiving, then it won't happen because forgiveness is a choice we make despite our feelings. Forgiveness

75

needs to be a conscious decision we make even in the middle of a storm of hurtful emotions pressing in on us from every direction.

You may be shouting at this book (at us really) saying: *"You don't know what they did to me! You don't know how they treated my child! You have no idea how much they hurt me and how I've been carrying this for years. You have no idea so don't lecture me!"*

We do know what it means to be deeply hurt by someone whom we trusted. Our testimony is that in our anger and pain towards the individual, we would not have come out the other side into freedom, (which we have done), unless we had made the decision to forgive. We can therefore empathize with people who are struggling with the deep pain of offence and betrayal, and so do not belittle anyone's situation in any way. We can testify however that forgiveness is the medicine to deal with the offence that's causing us pain.

Forgiveness _is_ Forgetting

The old adage *'I've forgiven but I've not forgotten'* is not helpful, because genuine forgiveness makes the choice not only to lay aside the offence, but also *to leave it behind*. We know someone whose mother-in-law made a written record of the offences her in-law kids committed against her so that others would know in the future. Thankfully she recognized for herself how damaging that was, and so got rid of the list before her death. It is easy to get offended, but the only way to build a relationship that can grow is to let go of past hurts. Holding on to *any part* of an offence leaves the door open for the resentment, the bitterness, and the anger we thought we'd dealt with, to creep back in at a later date and cause further problems. All of it needs to be forgiven *and* forgotten. We will finish this chapter with a testimony to the power of forgiveness:

"My relationship with my mother-in-law has taught me many things, especially the need to forgive. Over the years I have had to forgive a number of things - the way she speaks to me and about me, her lack of respect for cultural differences, her need to be the center of attention, as well as trying to put pressure regarding when we should visit. Whether she realized it or not, she saw me as a rival for her son's affection and instead of embracing me she has effectively driven me away. It has caused misery and many tears over the years, as well as having a knock-on effect on how my children view her and their relationship with her. I can't point the finger however and say it was solely her fault. I have also made mistakes and now realize that during the early years of my marriage 'I gave as good as I got' where my mother-in-law was concerned - which wasn't helpful.

However, as I matured and saw the effect the bad relationship was having on all of our family, I decided I needed to do things differently. This included changing my attitude towards her and choosing to forgive her for all the things she had said and done. Each time something new came up I have had to choose to forgive afresh and sometimes this has been extremely hard to do.

Over the years I have made a great deal of effort to show my willingness to put past problems behind us. Unfortunately my mother-in-law holds on very tightly to the past and as a result our relationship is not a good one. As things stand there is a politeness and cordiality between us but no warmth, which I do find sad. Not only have I missed out on having a good relationship with my mother-in-law, but our children have also missed out on a loving grandparent relationship. I've also come to recognize that had I not made the decision to keep on forgiving, then things would certainly be much worse than they are. It would have been far easier for me to say 'why bother', but I know that my decision to forgive no matter what has benefitted me greatly. It means I don't get worked up and upset about things that ultimately I have no control over. It means that I am free to stay happy whatever she has said and done. This doesn't mean I don't care, but it does mean I don't let it bother me anymore."

Whether you are a daughter-in-law, a mother-in-law, or any other individual in the in-law relationship, your decision to forgive is vitally important. Not only will it benefit you personally, it will also benefit the rest of the family. Things may not be perfect, especially to start with, but forgiveness does mean things will improve in one way or another and that the path to full reconciliation becomes easier.

Questions to Consider

Forgiveness is such a vital, yet personal issue that you need to think carefully about how to approach this matter as you consider the following questions. If it becomes obvious that you need to deal with past issues by either asking for, or extending forgiveness, be courageous and take the necessary steps required to heal past hurts.

1. Do you need to forgive someone? Difficult though it may be, you are free to make the choice if you so desire.

2. Do you need to *talk* to someone about how they have offended you? (Keep in mind they may be totally unaware they have upset you). Simply talking to them about what they said or did can become a bridge to repairing the relationship.

3. Do you need to *ask* someone to forgive you? Are you aware that you offended someone by something you said or did? Again, you have as much freedom to *ask* for forgiveness, as you do to *give* forgiveness to someone else.

Chapter 9

Third Medley

Don't Take Sides

Our children have jokingly said on a number of occasions how I take sides with our son or daughter-in-law, rather than taking sides with them when it comes to disagreements or having a different view on something. If I'm honest, there probably is some truth in what they say! It's not because my son or daughter-in-law are always right - it's because I have a soft spot for them both. I don't want to see them outnumbered by their spouse, as well as their parents-in-law when there's a disagreement!

Although the issues I'm referring to here from my own experience are trivial and would not undermine the relationship, I am aware it's something that I can't afford to ignore. This is especially true if a much bigger or more serious issue were to arise. We need to make sure we are impartial and are able to contribute in a way that guards the best interest of both our child, as well as their spouse equally. Continual favoritism towards our child over their spouse, or the other way around, can damage the in-law relationship.

I heard the story of a young couple who decided to have a 'trial separation' because of on-going difficulties in their marriage. During this time of separation the mother took every opportunity to tell her son all the things she disliked about her daughter in-law. This was extremely short sighted because the young couple decided to get back together again. The mother's personal feelings and opinions had now placed her in a *worse* position with regard to the in-law relationship than it was before! It was going to be even more of an uphill struggle for her now because she had fallen into the trap of trying to influence what her son thought about his wife in an attempt to make things easier for herself.

An approach we would have advised would have been to give her son the freedom he needed so that he could come to his own conclusions, rather than trying to influence him with her thoughts and prejudices. Unfortunately she allowed *her own personal agenda* to overtake her. She would have done well by actively encouraging her son to work towards a solution that was going to bring the best outcome *for the young married couple first and foremost,* and to keep quiet regarding her own personal preferences. After all, it was the son who would be more affected with the consequences of his decision in the longer term, not the mother.

Ensure Confidentiality

The importance of making sure we don't share information that has been given to us in confidence cannot be over-stated. Not keeping conversations private by sharing them with others, even with other family members, is called 'gossiping'. Nobody wants a gossiping parent-in-law! When we are seen as a safe place to share thoughts, plans, or concerns, it gives our in-law children the confidence they need to come to us for advice about anything, because they won't be worried by what will happen to the information they're prepared to trust us with.

It may be (for whatever reason) that we are the only place they feel they can share in confidence. If we then show ourselves to be untrustworthy, our in-law kids won't have *any* avenue to discuss and explore what may be an extremely important decision they have to make. They may then even end up making wrong decisions. Relationships can be severely damaged by not keeping a confidence, so it needs to be something all of us should be aware of so that our in-law relationships can be strengthened, not weakened.

Learn From Each Other

All of us to some degree or another have been shaped to do things 'our way'. As the older ones in the relationship, the parents-in-law can mistakenly think their way is the best way, which is not always true. Our way of doing things is the best way *we know* for doing something, but we need to be open to learning there may actually be a better way than ours. This includes learning from the generation below.

Our children (and we include our son-in-law and daughter-in-law in this) have very different views and ideas on certain issues than we do. Over the past few years we have learned to be open to them in order to learn from them, which has helped bring an understanding to us on various issues that has proved helpful. As well as being open to their viewpoints and opinions, we also need to be humble enough to sometimes ask for their advice on certain issues. If it's good advice then we need to take it, but even if we don't end up taking their advice, the fact that we've asked in the first instance will give them the confidence that we respect their opinion. This becomes a win-win situation for everybody!

Parents-in-law have a lot to give - it's just what happens when you've been around a bit longer! We can make the mistake however of thinking that we know everything, and that we don't need to grow any more. All of us need to continue to learn new things, and there is no reason why we can't do this from our children and their spouses. This type of openness to learn from one another helps the relationship grow in respect and understanding.

Don't Compare

If you have more than one child you will already know how different they can be. They will have different personalities, the way they live their lives and what they value most will be different, as well as their goals and ambitions.

Every parent has learned over the years how important it is not to compare their children, but this is just as important once they are married. If you have more than one set of in-law children, it is important to accept the differences between each couple, and to love them equally for who they are. Comparing in-law couples has the potential to damage the relationship we have with each one, as well as potentially damaging the relationship they have with each other as siblings if they see any favoritism creeping in.

Engage When Invited

Relationships grow when people spend time together, so we need to be aware of how important it is not to decline an invitation from our children-in-law too often. There are times when our reasons for declining are genuine, but if we consistently refuse because we simply can't be bothered, then we miss valuable opportunities to grow the relationship. Refusing an invite for no good reason makes a statement to the young couple that the relationship is not important us.

Questions to Consider

---

1. What have you learned about yourself, or about your in-law children from this chapter? Even if it is as simple as the chapter encouraging you that you are already doing a number of these things well, make a note of it.

2. Make a list of what you appreciate about your in-law children. Then find opportunities to share with them the various ways they encourage you. If you are brave enough to ask, get *them* to share with you the ways that you as a parent-in-law are an encouragement to them.

Chapter 10

Be Welcoming

I remember the first time I met my father-in-law. It was a miserable and dark winter's night, and I had just driven on my own for two hours from my parents' house. I was met by my (then) boyfriend, followed by a man who greeted me with a lovely smile and a joke about Fort Knox - because of the number of locks he needed to open to let me in. His warmth immediately put me at ease. I believe the foundation for the lovely relationship I had with him before he became ill with dementia was laid that first night we met, when he made me feel so welcome.

First impressions are very important, and so being welcoming at our first meeting with a prospective in-law child needs to be emphasized. It is a true statement that we don't get a second chance to make a first impression. Even if we have some reservations regarding the suitability of our child's new boyfriend / girlfriend, we have to put those to one side for the sake of the relationship. Our priority should be to welcome our child's choice of partner and provide an environment where they will feel at home.

A True Story

A couple shared with us regarding the welcome awaiting them when they first went to visit her parents in Northern Ireland. Their visit was at the height of the Northern Ireland troubles in the 1980's. The journey there was not an easy one - the train from the ferry port was full of football fans singing sectarian songs and generally making everybody else on the train feel very uncomfortable. The boyfriend felt extremely intimidated because of his easily recognizable English accent, worrying what would happen if someone started a conversation with him.

Once they were off the train, they were relieved to see the girl's father waiting for them at the station. Unfortunately, rather than taking them back to the safety of their home, the father proceeded to take him (them) on a sightseeing tour of some of the then roughest parts of Belfast. The tour included showing him paramilitary murals, burned out houses, and checkpoints. Most of the areas on this improvised tour were regarded as 'no-go' areas at the time. Whether this was a deliberate attempt by the father to try to frighten the culturally alien Englishman from getting any closer to his Irish daughter nobody knows. If it was, it proved unsuccessful, because the couple have now been married for over 30 years.

Considering Others

Being welcoming means we make a conscious effort to help the individual feel at ease. It includes making sure we don't allow any potential prejudices to cloud us from giving them the welcome they're hoping to receive. It is really important not to *"judge a book by its cover"* because appearances can often be deceiving. Someone with a loud personality can be a challenge to someone who is the quieter type, and vice versa. Our experience has been that different personalities can get on extremely well in the in-law relationship provided they accept and value their differences.

Recovering 'The First Impression'

But what if our first meeting has long been and gone and it didn't go well - what do we do then? Well, there are a couple of things we can do.

Firstly, look at what we've learned from the experience so far. Was our attitude a contributing factor to the relationship not blossoming - or are we happy that we could not have done any more? We need to at least *consider* whether we fell short in our welcome or not. If we do recognize we were at fault, then we need to acknowledge it and take remedial action through chatting things through and even offering an apology if necessary. Showing humility when we get things wrong speaks volumes to the in-law children, and goes a long way towards building a strong relationship.

The second thing we can do is to make sure the next time is an opportunity for a *fresh start*. We may need to change our behavior, change our attitude, and be warmer. That will lead us to be more welcoming when we next meet up with our in-law children. There's no need to go over the top, but at least if we start to allow some warmth to come through it will be a step in the right direction. As the in-law child experiences some friendliness (in the same way I felt it from my father-in-law), they will hopefully be encouraged to reciprocate the affection. So, if we've messed it up first time round, we don't need to despair because there is always the possibility of doing things better the next time!

Nothing Will Change If We Don't Change

If we carry on doing things the wrong way, then nothing will change. If however we try to initiate changes from our side, at least there is the potential for things to improve. It is important we don't beat ourselves up for past mistakes. Strong relationships are built between people who value the relationship to the extent they are willing to learn from their mistakes and then work together to sort out differences. All of us are on the journey of learning -

the only difference is that we're all being challenged in different ways, at different times, and to varying degrees.

To Hug or Not To Hug?

Being welcoming means being warm and loving towards someone because we want them to feel at ease. If the person is from a family where words were harsh, hugs were few, and encouragement lacking then this will be a new and unfamiliar situation for them. This is even more of a reason to be welcoming because they need to know they will be loved and accepted by us in their new extended family. They may not be comfortable receiving hugs and kisses in the way we're used to giving them, so this may take a little working through. Conversely, as parents-in-law we ourselves may not be that free to either give or receive hugs and kisses. So if we're greeted by an enthusiastic 'good to see you' which involves a hug, then for the sake of the relationship go with it!

It is important to be sensitive to the individual because hugging may be a new language some people need to learn - *but only if they want to*. If you suspect this to be the case then the best way forward is as we've mentioned previously - slow and steady so that the new person does not feel overwhelmed. After all, the whole point is to make them feel welcomed and at ease, not to make them feel uncomfortable. If we're not sure what the situation is as far as giving a hug is concerned it is okay to ask permission - *'are you okay with me giving you a hug?'* From personal experience I can say that slowly, the person joining the family will begin to appreciate the hug, and even get to the place of being the one who initiates them.

Giving Time is Welcoming

Personally, I feel welcomed when someone has time for me, and takes an interest in what I have to say. It can be very off-putting when someone gives the impression they are in a hurry, or even in the middle of a conversation they start looking around to see who else has come into the room. It's not that I'm boring - it's just the other person is rude by communicating there is something (or someone) more important they would rather be engaging with! Let's make sure therefore that we fully engage with the person we're listening to, so that they feel valued and appreciated.

In closing this chapter it may be fitting to say that the definition of welcoming is *'to greet in a polite or friendly way; be glad to entertain or receive; react with pleasure or approval'[1]*. If our desire is to build a loving relationship with our in-law children then this definition of what it means to welcome someone speaks for itself. Obviously the importance of giving a warm welcome is not to be limited to the first meeting alone - we need to be consistent at being welcoming each time we get together with our in-law children. As we do that, the rewards that come from growing the in-law relationship will be worth it!

[1] www.oxforddictionaries.com

Questions to Consider

1. What sort of things do you currently do that make your child and their spouse feel they are welcome?

2. Can you think of anything else that you could *start* doing to make them feel even more welcome?

3. Have a think about it, is there anything you are currently doing or saying that may give your child and spouse the impression they are *not* welcome? Do you need to change anything so that they are not in any doubt you are pleased to see them?

Chapter 11

Closing Medley

Avoid Applying Pressure

The relationship between the young married couple is more important than the relationship we have with them as parents-in-law. It is important to remember this in order to give them space to develop their relationship, and not put any undue expectations or pressures on them as far as the relationship they have with us is concerned.

As parents-in-law we need to avoid applying *'the pressure of expectation'* on our child and their spouse. Instead, we need to give them a full freedom to make their own decisions and choices. When we apply pressure (knowingly or unknowingly), even though the young couple may conform to the request in order to keep the peace, it can lead to resentment and eventually strife. The strife can be between us and them, but worse still between the young couple themselves as a result of split loyalties.

Christmas is one example we can give from our own lives. This is a time when there is often an expectation on young couples to do what the parents (in-law) want them to do. Our approach has been to give our in-law children a full freedom to choose what they want to do at Christmas - without making them feel guilty if their choice is not what we were hoping for. This has meant there have been occasions when there was just the two of us having a quiet Christmas Day together. Though it would have been a lot more exciting to spend Christmas with our kids and their spouses, it was the price we were willing to pay so they could have the freedom to do things the way they wanted to. We avoided putting them under any duress or obligation to conform to our preferences, and also made it clear they weren't to feel guilty for choosing to do what they wanted.

Reaping The Rewards of Giving Freedom

Having given them the freedom in the early years, what we now see is that they *want* to spend Christmas with us - either at our home, or we get invited to theirs. Because we've always given them the choice, and continue to do so, we're encouraged to know this is *their* decision - we're not invited out of a sense of duty or obligation on their part. Giving them this independence has helped tremendously in the bigger picture of the relationship we have with both sets of in-law children, because they have come to learn we don't put pressure on them. Hopefully this experience from our own lives will help others see how important it is not to pressure our in-law kids to conform, but rather to give them a full freedom which is free from expectancy, as well as guilt.

The example we've given is only one area where parents-in-law have the potential to put expectations on their child and spouse. Pressure from the in-laws can come in different ways and from various directions, so we thought we would include the following testimony on how one husband recalls the pressure he felt when visiting his girlfriend's parents:

"During the time we started going out with each other, I would go and visit her at her parent's house. It was quite a small house and to prevent any uncomfortable discussion about sleeping arrangements, I usually slept outside on their veranda. Even though this was an unconventional location for a guest to sleep, especially one who was increasingly looking as if he would become part of the family, it wasn't really a problem because secretly I quite liked the chance to camp out and have a bit of peace and quiet.

Anyway, what troubled me more was the morning chat I'd invariably end up having with my future father-in-law. I'm the sort of person who needs a few minutes to come round, drink at least one cup of coffee, and ideally have a cold shower before I'm ready to face the day. But it was as if he would lie in wait to corner me as I came back into the house. I had hardly opened my eyes and there he was, wearing a barely decent silky dressing gown. I was greeted with an enthusiastic "Good Morning!" and the fact that he called me by my full Christian name somehow brought an official and business-like feel to the encounter. Then he would go on to say "How was your night? Alright?"

Once the formality of the initial greeting was out of the way, he would then get down to the serious business at hand. "Now, I've been meaning to ask you about your timescale with regard to my daughter. I mean, I don't mean to jump on you but I was just wondering what your intentions may be with reference to your courtship?"

Even though we are now married, the morning inquisitions have continued, though I must admit it has become easier over the years to get used to the silky dressing gown. The subjects of these early morning 'chats' however still catch me out because they can vary from anything such as theology, my career plans, children, all the way over to how bad my last deal on car insurance was.

Though the encounters were awkward especially in the early days, somehow I managed to come through them and choose to believe he has our best interests at heart. Many a young suitor may well have been put off by such prying inquisition, but thankfully I wasn't."

Use Your Time Together Wisely

When the opportunity to spend time with our now married children and their spouses is presented to us, we always try to *think ahead* as to how best to make the most of the time we have with them. Often it's a time to simply sit, relax, have a coffee and just catch up on what's happening in their lives. Going for walks and having food together are also things we personally enjoy doing with our family, as is having fun with the grandchildren. There is no formula to how we should spend our time with them, because different people enjoy different things. The message we're trying to communicate however is to be intentional, so that we can make the most of our time together.

Grandchildren

Even though this book is specifically aimed at the relationship between parents and their adult in-law children, a thought needs to be given to the issue of how this relationship can be affected by grandchildren.

The *subject* of grandchildren has the potential to become a disruptive issue in the in-law relationship - even before a child actually appears on the scene. It's not the grandchild themselves that is the problem, but the *issue* some parents / parents-in-law make of grandchildren. Some parents-in-law unfortunately start to put pressure on their kids with regard to when they are going to start a family. They may come straight out with the question, or they may drop subtle hints every now and again. By doing this, they are inadvertently placing an expectation on the young couple, which can be interpreted by them as pressure to start a family when they're not ready to do so. Worse still is the fact that it is an *intrusion* into the private life of the young couple - something the parents lost the right to when their child got married. If the young couple do not bring up the subject, neither should we as parents-in-law, because we don't always know the bigger picture of what's going on in their lives.

The other important point to mention with regard to grandchildren is to *never air grievances, or worse still have an argument with our in-law children, in front of grandchildren.* If this happens, not only does it damage the in-law relationship - it has the potential also to damage the relationship we have with our grandchildren. Children are especially loyal to their parents, and so they will see us through the eyes of the disagreement - someone who is hostile towards their parents. Negative experiences of witnessing a heated disagreement between their parents and grandparents is something that leaves the child confused, and doesn't model how loving relationships should be conducted - so we need to avoid it at all cost.

Respect The Other Parents-in-Law

Though we may not realize it, how we relate to the other set of parents-in-law is actually very important to the relationship we have with the young couple. We should never criticize the other set of parents-in-law to our child or their spouse, even when it is obvious their attitude or behavior falls short. Neither should we contribute to someone else's conversation that may be criticizing the other set of parents-in-law.

A poor relationship between respective parents-in-law can not only directly affect their married children, it can also affect their grandchildren and leave a negative impression that is difficult to shake off. The following testimony is proof of how as a child, this woman's experience witnessing the breakdown in relationship that had occurred between her parent's in-laws has left its mark on her.

"My grandparents (my parent's parents) on either side did not get on. Both mother-in-laws were strong willed and opinionated women who disliked each other intensely. This caused a great deal of tension in our house when we were children and made family gatherings impossible. My parents each felt loyalty to their own parents rather than each other and this caused many arguments at home. My

parents had a poor marriage anyway and separated on more than one occasion. Their parents often made the situation worse by seeing no fault in their own child and would put all the blame on my other parent. Each of my parents was simply tolerated by their respective parents-in-law, and seen as outsiders to their own family.

On one occasion when my parents had separated we were living with my mum's parents for a few months. My father's parents sent some money to help look after us. However, they chose to wrap it in toilet paper. What should have been a kind gesture was interpreted as the ultimate insult and my mother's parents never forgave them. This affected me as a child as I felt torn between two different families. I never remember seeing both sets of parents-in-law in the same room even though they lived no more than five miles apart."

This is just one story of how a poor relationship between respective parents-in-laws affected a family over three generations. It directly affected both sets of in-laws; the young married couple; as well as their grandchildren. Even if it is difficult to get on with the other set of parents-in-law, the least we must do is to ensure that we do nothing to undermine the young couple's relationship with them. We can see from this testimony that the biggest losers are not the parents-in-law who don't get on. It was the young couple who lost out most, because they were constantly torn between their respective parents. To what extent this contributed to the break down in the couple's marriage no-one will ever know, but the extra stress and friction between the two sets of parents-in-law will undoubtedly have played some part in it.

Closing Remarks

None of us have perfected the in-law relationship, because it's one of life's journeys that as parents, we have to learn along the way - there's no other approach on offer to us. It is a truly unique relationship, and add to this the fact that no two in-law relationships are the same, it's no wonder it brings such a plethora of challenges! But we need to balance that by recognizing the rewards this relationship brings are also unique, and are so special that it is worth the hard work we have to put in so we can experience them.

One of the aims of this book is to *add* to the excellent work that countless parents-in-law are already doing - it's to give them a few more arrows in their quiver so they can become even stronger parents-in-law. Another aim of the book is to help lay a foundation for those who are just starting off as new parents-in-law. Our hope is that we have been able to achieve at least some of these objectives as we've shared with you some of the things we've learned over our forty-year journey. Continue being resolute so you can come through the challenges; be humble enough to admit and then learn from your mistakes; but most importantly enjoy the distinct pleasures that only this unique and special relationship can bring.

Enjoy the journey!

Questions to Consider

1. Can you think of any particular chapters in the book which have resonated with your situation? Do you need to revisit those chapters to get the most out of them?

2. Look back at the responses you gave to some of the questions. Is there anything you have made a note of that needs to be put into practice without delay?

3. Write down the hopes you have for your in-law relationship, as well as some of the small things you are already doing that are taking you closer to your goal.

Made in the USA
Las Vegas, NV
26 March 2024

87828551R00069